BEYOND BATTERIES
A MOTHER'S HURRICANE
SURVIVAL GUIDE

By Karen Grossman, VHS (Veteran Hurricane Survivor)

I0411387

Dedication

This book is dedicated to all people who sacrifice to protect their families and homes against dangerous storms.

This book is also dedicated to my personal anchor in a storm. See, Matthew 14:30-33.

30 But when he (Peter) saw the wind, he was afraid and, beginning to sink, cried out, "Lord, save me!"31 Immediately Jesus reached out his hand and caught him. "You of little faith," he said, "why did you doubt?"32 And when they climbed into the boat, the wind died down. 33 Then those in the boat worshiped him, saying, "Truly you are the Son of God."

Acknowledgements

Many thanks to my husband, David Grossman, for his support and encouragement during the writing of this book, and for being by my side through life's storms since 1982. Thanks to my children Caroline Grace and Matthew Charles, for inspiring me to write this book. Thanks also to my parents, Fred and Sylvia Foy, who instilled in me the importance of family and being well prepared. Finally, thanks to my sister, Linda Foy, whose enthusiasm helped me to finish what I started.

Table of Contents

Prologue

Hurricane David

Growing up in Miami, Florida, hurricanes were things that happened in other places. In 1979, however, Hurricane David, a category 5 storm, was forecast to strike Miami. My family lived in a stucco house with floor to ceiling thin glass jalousie windows. This style of window was designed to make the most of breezes before air conditioning was common. Of course the last thing one wants in a hurricane is to make the most of the breeze. We knew these windows would shatter to thousands of shards if they were not covered. My father bought a lot of plywood, and planned where each piece would go.

The day David approached, in pre-storm, super-heated humidity, I helped my father hoist plywood over each window of the house, gripping the rough edges as he drilled into the wall. Hours later I was exhausted and tomato-faced, but all our windows were covered. We retreated into our tomb-dark house to await the storm.

In bed that night I listened expectantly to updates on my clock/radio. I strained to hear the first raindrop. Nothing happened. It soon became apparent that the storm was passing to our north. All our preparations were for nothing. While a normal person would be relieved after dodging a bullet, I was downcast. The thought of removing all that plywood added dread to my disappointment. This is my dad and I in front of our living room jalousie windows.

Hurricane Andrew

Fast forward to August 1992. I was a young bride living in a townhouse in Kendall, a suburb of Miami located inland, well out of the flood zone. My husband and a friend had gone to the Florida Keys to fish for the weekend. I received a call from my mother-in-law about an approaching hurricane named "Andrew." She was concerned that my husband may be on a boat in the Keys. Until the call, I had not even noticed the news coverage of the hurricane. Who can trust the weather reports anyway? Nevertheless, I reached my husband, who said he would monitor things and decide if he should come back.

In the Keys, there is only one road out. If you wait too long to evacuate, you are not allowed to tow a boat because it slows everyone down. So, my husband and his friend started trying to find out what evacuation orders were being issued. They stopped at a gas station, where suddenly people hurried to line up for gas.

Pre-storm panic is a strange communal phenomenon. Everyone moves very quickly, and the slow-paced vibe in the Keys made the contrast more obvious. When you see others are focused on lining up for gas and hitting the ATM, you don't want to be left without. Soon everyone's anxiety ramps up. My husband and his friend decided they should head back to Miami while they could still tow the boat.

I had been home gathering flashlights, unaware of the spreading panic. Then I decided to head to the grocery store for non-perishables in case our power went out. As soon as I pulled into the parking lot, I saw masses of people, no shopping carts, and bag boys handing out boxes to use to carry groceries. I got a box and hurried inside. There was near pandemonium in the store. People grabbed bottled water, canned goods, bread, and peanut butter. I joined the fray indiscriminately grabbing things for my box which I would not normally buy such as snack cakes, canned soup, all manner of crackers, and the remnants of the store's bottled water supply.

After waiting in a long line I got extra cash and returned home, my heart beating at a much faster rate than when I had set out. I called my husband to let him know how crazy things were getting. He downplayed people's panic, blaming the media for over-dramatizing the coming storm. I reminded myself of Hurricane David and how it failed to live up to my expectations.

Meanwhile, friends who lived in a condo on Key Biscayne asked if they could ride out the storm with us. Key Biscayne is surrounded by water, only accessible by bridge. They wanted to bring their art and valuables with them in case their place was destroyed. Of course we obliged. My mother-in-law also decided to leave her Pinecrest home (a neighborhood located close to Biscayne Bay) and stay the night in our house.

Our friends arrived and we discussed the latest newspaper headline: "**BIGGER, STRONGER, CLOSER**" warned the front page in large black letters. I started getting caught up in the news coverage. One station reported any loose rocks would become like bullets when the wind arrived. I saw our courtyard, completely covered in loose Chattahoochee stones.

We had no shutters or plywood to cover our ten sliding glass doors and second story windows. Still, we reassured ourselves it would not matter because we were located inland, and were not ordered to evacuate. I tried to remain calm, but my anxiety was building.

The five of us slept lightly that night, until around 4 a.m. The first thing I noticed was my ears popping as if I were in a plane. The fast drop in air pressure made me feel a little sick. Soon the winds loudly shook the foundation of the house. Our "Plan A" had been to get in the master bedroom's walk-in closet and sit on the floor if things got bad. Within minutes of the first gust we all went into the closet. No sooner had we gotten in, the attic entrance panel in the closet ceiling was sucked up, and a shower of pink, itchy insulation rained down on us. We dashed out of the closet, brushing off insulation.

We decided "Plan B" would be an interior bathroom downstairs. As my husband stood at the top of our stairs he paused. Despite all the windows being closed, he could feel wind in the house. We decided it was too risky to go downstairs should the glass doors break while we were trying to make it to the bathroom. "Plan C" became the five of us stumbling into a very small master bathroom, which connected by another door to the guest room. We ran in so fast we were in no particular order and I sat down on the floor separated from my husband. He said "Oh no you're not next to me!" but my mother-in-law, seated by my husband, retorted, "You have your mother!"

We also had a radio with us in the bathroom and a small air mattress over our heads. The mirror glued to the wall above the sink started to bend as the house shook. The entire house seemed fluid, and the wind noise became indescribably loud. People often say a tornado sounds like an approaching freight train. Andrew sounded like screaming lions, not gradually getting louder like an approaching train, but circling and closing tightly upon you as they lunge from every direction—it was evil. After hunkering down a few moments, we heard glass shatter. Things outside the bathroom were breaking, crashing, and tearing. I stole glances under the air mattress at my husband, who was braced against the door leading to the guest room.

I was overcome by a sense of smallness in the midst of the storm's fury. Being at the mercy of such a powerful destructive force was a completely new life experience, and it exceeded all expectations. It was sustained fright.

Radio updates by now famed weatherman Brian Norcross let us know when strong storm bands were nearing us. Each time one approached, my husband's friend would moan, "oh nooooo." I wondered how long it would be before the mirror shattered, or our house fell completely apart. After a seeming eternity of noise, the wind died down.

My husband ventured out through the master bedroom, which looked just as we had left it. Then he opened the door to the top of the stairs. His first impression was that the hall was very bright. He looked up and saw the sky. Part of our roof had been completely ripped off by the storm. Our guest bedroom window had broken, and one wall of that room had fallen to the first floor. Debris was everywhere. Oddly, a picture hanging above our living room couch remained on the wall, not even crooked.

Everything our friends had brought for safekeeping had been stored in the guest room and was destroyed. Their small car had been pushed around a corner. All I could think was at least it is over. We got through it. Then I went outside, and realized it would not be over for a long time. No power pole remained, and every leaf had been torn from the few trees that survived. The world was brown, debris littered the ground, dead birds were strewn about, and we were in a daze. It looked like a scene from "Apocalypse."

None of the other townhouses in our pod lost their roof, so our home became something of an attraction. Strangers just started walking through the house and looking up at the sky. At first I was angry, (do I know you?) as I was sweeping chunks of drywall out of what was left of our house, but I realized these neighbors were just in shock. Over and over I swept the same area of tile as dust, glass, and drywall seemed to reappear after I carried the dust pan to the trash can.

My husband's friend kept complaining that he couldn't find the belt to his velour robe. Hearing him I realized I had swept it away with the debris, not knowing what it was at the time, but I refused to own up to it. I continued to sweep as he searched the debris for his belt. How could he be so concerned about his dumb belt when I was literally picking up the pieces of our home? Years later I did confess to his wife that I had trashed his soggy velour robe belt.

We did what we could to clean up, and sat outside on top of coolers. The sound of helicopters came some hours later, and then the rumors that whole communities were gone, and other (mostly true) horror stories. Streets were unrecognizable because landmarks and road signs were gone. I reached my parents through a neighbor with a working phone and assured them we were okay, but we needed to cover the holes in our house. Somehow my father, who ran a claims adjusting company in Orlando, found a truck to locate us, board up the window and tarp the roof. To this day I am amazed that they found us.

The days that followed were surreal. We waited for our mail at the post office (since it could not be delivered due to debris) while National Guardsmen with machine guns stood watch. People had handguns in their belts to defend and secure what was left of their property.

My sister-in-law lived on a lake in Cutler Ridge, a neighborhood rumored to be hard-hit. After not hearing from her for three days, my husband borrowed a motorcycle and headed south, weaving in and around downed trees and debris. He ultimately found her alive and well. She had ridden out the storm with a girlfriend and a pot-bellied pig. Although her house was damaged, it remained standing. Other houses on the lake were completely demolished.

In the weeks after the storm, people found ways to entertain themselves without power or cell phones. Our first child, a daughter, was born almost exactly nine months after the storm, and was part of a 30% increase in births that month. She was born on the day of the first tropical depression of the next season.

Here is David Grossman, my husband, before Hurricane Andrew.

His smile shows we felt fully prepared. He is wearing plastic

protective goggles and gripping a flashlight. We used the

mattress to cover the sliding doors in the master bedroom.

This shows the second story of our townhouse, and the top landing of our stairs after Hurricane Andrew. The bathroom door of the small master bathroom is behind the door in the forefront.

This shows the hole in our roof after the hurricane.

Hurricane Erin

In the summer of 1995 I was in my last trimester of pregnancy with our second child when Hurricane Erin approached Florida. It was the first Hurricane since Andrew to strike the United States. Being in my last trimester, my doctor required me to ride out the storm at the hospital. Something about the falling air pressure is known to bring on labor. Something important to keep in mind if you are pregnant!

The hallways of the hospital were lined with pregnant women. We passed the time sitting on the floor on blankets, wondering whether a baby, a hurricane, or both would come before the night was over. Fortunately the hurricane passed to our north. I was not aware of anyone who went into early labor.

2005: Katrina and Others

The most active hurricane season in recorded history was in 2005. That year, Hurricane Katrina first made landfall in Miami before striking Louisiana and breaking Hurricane Andrew's record of destruction. As it came through Miami, we only lost fencing and screening, feeling fortunate to experience minimal damage. We were horrified by the flooding, deaths and lack of appropriate post-storm aid to the victims in Louisiana. Lessons learned from that catastrophe could fill volumes.

My family rode out so many storms during the 2005 season I vowed to fix up the house and move to another, less hurricane prone state. The kids repeatedly missed school as "Hurricane Days" were declared. I fantasized about selling the house the following February, when naïve snowbirds flock to the area for the best weather of the year. We are all susceptible to storm amnesia when the weather is beautiful, and we have remained in the "sunshine" state.

Hurricane "Superstorm" Sandy

As of this writing, the effects of Sandy are still being experienced by thousands of coastal residents in the northeast. I know of people who lost their homes, their jobs, and their cars, as all were wiped out by the storm. Our neighbors to the north deal with the low limits of flood insurance (many times maxing out at $250,000) that left them with irreplaceable property damage.

Preparation Limits

Large Hurricanes such as Andrew, Katrina, and Sandy, prove the point that sometimes all the preparation in the world will not protect your property from the fury of a powerful storm. Roofs blow off properly shuttered homes, flood waters flow into unpredicted areas, falling trees kill people, and power lines ignite or electrocute. In short, storms are dangerous, unpredictable and deadly.

After a major storm you are on your own at least for the first 48 to 72 hours. No emergency vehicles or police are likely to respond to you. No stores, no gas, no cash machines, and no water can be bought. Your family's survival and comfort will depend on what you have done to prepare before the storm.

The goal of this book is to help mothers do the most they can to protect themselves, their family and their home as a storm approaches. It includes the little things, "beyond batteries," that the weatherman does not discuss. I hope your preparations will make your family a little bit safer and more comfortable when the inevitable storm is near.

Before the Storm

Laundry

You won't hear the weatherman tell you to get the laundry started, but that is one of the first things I make sure is done as a storm approaches. Your washing machine will be out of commission for perhaps two weeks. Therefore, make sure you have everything you would pack if you were going on a two-week vacation. You need clean clothes, and every towel in the house. Towels can prevent water intrusion during a storm and are essential for clean up after a storm. A clothesline for hanging wet towels after the storm is also helpful. Laundry takes time and can be an ongoing activity the day or two before the storm. Leave a stack of big towels by doors so they are handy in case water comes in under the door.

Cash and Gas

Two places long lines quickly develop are the gas station and the ATM. Both are likely to run out before the storm. Fill up all your cars with gas. A siphon can be helpful should you want to transfer gas from your car to use in a generator. Bring extra gas containers to fill up for use with a generator or as an emergency supply if your car runs out of gas.

Next, visit your bank or ATM and get enough cash to last a few weeks. Try to get small bills. After the storm, cash is king and the ATMs do not work. Having cash may mean you get water or food for your family. You can also use it for fuel or to pay someone with a chainsaw to clear your yard or road.

Ideally you can delegate the gas and cash to another family member while you head to the grocery store.

Groceries

You need plenty of bottled water to stay hydrated in the heat and to stay clean. Buy all the water you can store. Buy cereal, boxed milk, and packaged breakfast bars. Coffee in single serving packs are a life-saver if you are caffeine-dependent. Paper plates, paper towels, cups and plastic utensils are needed to conserve water. Remember, no dishwasher if no power. Wet wipes are good for staying clean and germ free. Zippered plastic bags in all sizes can be used to safeguard important documents. Buy bread, peanut butter and any dry food you enjoy eating. Unless you have a power source, things like soup and ravioli will have to be consumed cold. Make sure you have a manual can opener. Think high nutrition and ease of preparation.

Make sure the gas grill has an extra propane tank. The day after the storm you can grill the defrosted meats from your freezer. Keep in mind that once roads open up you can usually drive a few hours and get out of the storm zone for a hot meal.

Coolers and Ice

Dig out all of your coolers and make ice. One easy way is to fill mixing bowls with water and freeze them. That results in blocks of ice that take longer to melt than the chunks of cubes you get in a store-bought bag of ice. The ice and coolers can be used to preserve unrefrigerated food and keep drinks cool.

Pay Bills

After a major storm, mail service takes a while to resume. If you have important bills that are about to come due, such as your mortgage, pay it before the storm. While many companies extend grace periods for customers affected by storms, it is another phone call and hassle you can avoid if you take care of major bills in advance.

Medications

Everyone in the household who takes prescription medicine should have a month's supply before the storm. Your local doctor may not be available to write or refill a prescription as the storm approaches. Everyone is busy making preparations to safeguard their family and property. Also make sure you have a good supply of over the counter medicine, and a well-stocked first aid kit.

Document your "Before" House

Use a camera to photograph your house "before" the storm. Include valuable items indoors, as well as the exterior of the home. Make sure to recharge your camera before the storm so you will be able to use it to document any damage after the storm.

Bug Spray , Trash Bags and Tarps

After hurricane Andrew, we had literally mountains of ants up against the plastic ant baits I kept in the house. A storm brings these insects inside, and you have to be ready to defend yourself and your food cache. Buy ant and roach spray. Be on the lookout for snakes after the storm, because they notoriously dislike the wet ground and can easily find their way into your home.

You can never have too many trash bags. The big, construction sized bags are good for yard debris. You will likely be using paper products to conserve your water supply, so you will have a lot of trash. Trash pick up will not be on its regular schedule after a storm. You want the thickest bags available to store garbage so it won't smell up the house, break open, or attract critters. The large bags can be cut to become tarps after the storm.

Tarping any area of your home exposed to rain after the storm can take a long time if you are waiting on FEMA or some other agency to come along with one. There are also some roofs FEMA will not tarp, such as metal roofs. If you have room to store it, purchase a large tarp and a roll of plastic sheeting to seal off your home from further damage after the storm.

Spray Paint

Fluorescent orange spray paint can be useful in communicating your family's needs to those patrolling by helicopter. Some people also spray paint the name of their insurance company on their house to be easily identified by adjusters dispatched to the storm area.

Gadgets

You know you will need flashlights and batteries. Batteries of all sizes are needed to power larger lanterns and flashlights. Provide each person in the household with their personal flashlight and battery supply. Reserve large lantern type flashlights for the kitchen table and family room. Don't use candles because of the risk of fire. Firefighters cannot respond during a hurricane.

If you are lucky enough to still have cell service after the storm, you will want to charge your phone. There are many chargers on the market designed for use in an emergency. If you have a car charger don't forget you can use it. There are also emergency radios with hand cranks or solar power strips that have a USB port for charging cell phones and other USB devices. Portable TVs only work if they are digitalized. A good battery powered radio is always helpful.

If you are able, a chain saw is an excellent tool to have for after the storm. You can clear the roadway, take limbs off of cars and roofs, and help your neighbors.

The most valuable gadget to have is also the most expensive: a generator. A large one can power most of your house while a small one can power smaller appliances. After numerous outages, we bought one of the large generators, as well as a smaller generator. The important thing to remember is generators operate on gasoline, so you have to stock up on enough gasoline prior to the storm to be able to run the generators for at least a few days. Also there is a real danger of carbon monoxide poisoning if the generator is not placed outdoors in a well-ventilated area. Finally, generators are very noisy. After a while the noise is more of a nuisance than the power outage. In my experience, the small Honda generator powered most of what we needed without using much gas. The large generator consumed so much fuel it hardly seemed worth powering everything in the house for a day.

One item many found necessary after Hurricane Andrew was a firearm. Personally I wouldn't want one around my house, but many people felt it was the most efficient way to protect their property after the storm. Police are scarce after a storm, and may not be able to respond or to even find you to respond if some unsavory characters are roaming the neighborhood and picking through debris.

Pets

If you are not in an evacuation zone, and plan to ride out the storm with your pet, make sure you have plenty of dog food, and a safe area for your pet within the house during the storm. Also obtain a crate in case you have to unexpectedly and quickly leave your house for safer ground. If you are in an evacuation zone, find out which shelters accept pets. Some vets will also board your pet during a hurricane.

Kids

Locate things that don't require electricity to entertain your children. Decks of cards, board games, books, coloring books, and other non-powered activities will help keep them busy. If you can give your children some responsibilities in storm preparation it may make them feel more in control and less stressed. Keeping their room organized with things off the floor will help when you are trying to get around the house with limited light. Pick up an inexpensive activity book at the grocery store to surprise them with after the storm. By and large, if you are calm about carrying out preparations, the children will take your cue and remain calm.

Property

If you are in a flood zone and have a two-story house, move valuable furniture to the second story in advance of the storm. If you are in a single story house, you may want to put valuable furniture or antiques up on cinder blocks to get them off the floor. Use the large plastic trash bags to cover TV's and computer equipment. Unplug as many items as possible, to reduce damage to your electronics during power surges and lightening strikes. Plastic zippered bags are useful for documents, books, or other smaller items susceptible to water damage.

Final Preparations

Charge everything that needs charging. Decide upon a friend or relative you will contact who can contact others after the storm. Turn down the air-conditioning so your house will be cool for a while after the power goes off. Take a nice long hot shower and blow dry your hair for the last time before the storm. Make sure the children have had their baths. Relax and monitor the weather news.

Evacuating

If you live in a flood zone or evacuation zone, it is often too late to leave by the time you are certain you want to evacuate. Storms are unpredictable, and can turn at the last minute. You will have to judge based on the size of the storm whether you want to leave town before evacuation orders are given. We once drove to Disney World to evacuate in advance of a hurricane. There were special hotel rates for evacuees and we ended up with an unplanned mini vacation. Despite the discount, it was also an unplanned budget-buster. The best option is to stay with friends or relatives outside of the storm cone, if possible.

If you are ordered to evacuate, leave. Things can get bad fast once the storm starts, and you do not want to put yourself or your family in danger. You also do not want to put emergency personnel at risk for having to rescue you because you didn't heed the evacuation warning. When you do evacuate, bring pillows, blankets, your homeowner's insurance and any other important documents such as passports, mortgages, computer passwords, car titles and anything else you want to safeguard. Documents left behind should be put in plastic bags or plastic containers. Valuables such as jewelry should also be taken in case damage to your house compromises the home's security.

Outside the Home

I have heard a joke summing up hurricane preparation as: gather your homeowner's insurance policy, open the windows, and go to Disney World. Before Andrew, that might have been decent advice. But these days deductibles are high and coverage is limited. Any damage to your home will result in huge expenses. The way policies are written now, it would take truly catastrophic damage before the insurance kicks in, and even then, much of your loss will be born by you. Therefore, take all steps you can afford to protect your property.

Bring loose objects inside. Lawn and patio furniture will be blown away or damaged if not secured. If you have shutters, use them over the windows. If you do not have shutters, obtain plywood cut to fit each window, and store these for future storms. If you don't have precut plywood, obtain either yourself or through and handy-person enough plywood to be cut to fit your windows. In a hurricane, once wind enters the home you will have a lot of damage. Remember that after all the windows are shuttered, your house will be very dark. I have seen some homeowners leave a small area un-shuttered so they can monitor the storm. Of course there is a risk that damage will occur to that vulnerable area.

Impact resistant windows are a good but large investment. It is nice to be able to see outside during the storm. You can also avoid the labor involved in shuttering all of your windows every time a storm approaches. These expensive windows can still be damaged during a storm, so to protect your investment and be even more secured, you may want to shutter the impact resistant windows.

If you have a garage bring the cars inside the garage and park them close to the garage door. Miami requires new garage doors to be impact resistant, but most doors are vulnerable to some damage in a storm.

If you have large trees on your property, have a local arborist or yard service thin out your tree. There is a particular way to trim trees so the wind can blow through the branches, making it less likely that the tree will fall down. An untrimmed tree, full of leaves and branches will bear the full brunt of the wind and will come down much easier than a trimmed tree. This is a preparation best done at the beginning of hurricane season, once a year.

During the Storm

Where to Be

If you have not evacuated, pick a spot in your house for your family to ride out the storm. Ideally, an interior room with no windows is safest. Unfortunately, no house I have ever lived in has had an interior room with no windows. Pick the room with the fewest or smallest windows, which are preferably shuttered, and set up your hunker down station there. Bring in pillows, blankets, battery operated lights and a good radio to monitor the storm.

Have another area of the house in mind where you will go to if the first area is damaged. Many people found a bathtub to be their safe haven in Hurricane Andrew. Even a fully shuttered house can be leveled if it is in the direct path of a powerful storm. Stick together as much as possible, even if everyone is uncomfortable in a small space. The storm won't last forever.

After the Storm

When to Come Out

Keep monitoring the storm on the radio weather station. When the eye of the storm passes over you, everything will get calm, and the sun may even shine. Do not go outside. Assess how your plan worked during the first part of the storm and make any adjustments necessary. Stay close to the place where you rode out the first half so you can get back there in a hurry.

Depending on where the storm passes, sometimes the eye will not come over you, and you will experience the outer bands of the storm for the duration of the system. In any event, after all the winds have died down, emerge from your secure area and stay within the house. An adult can do a quick assessment of the inside of the house and determine whether it is safe for everyone to come out.

Do not go outside immediately after the storm ends for a variety of reasons. Everyone will want to see what happened outside. The spectacle of trees on cars and houses, roofs torn off, or other damage gets everyone's attention. Despite curiosity, it is unsafe to immediately go outside after a storm.

First, power lines may be down and live, which causes a risk of electrocution to anyone standing near them. With all the debris, you may not be aware that you are near a downed power line.

Secondly, although the worst has passed, wind gusts can continue to occur. Against rain-soaked roots and weakened trees, more trees and branches are likely to come down. Falling trees are a common killer after a hurricane.

Finally, pets whose fences have blown down, and other animals (snakes and alligators) may unexpectedly turn up in your yard. These animals are already stressed and it is best to stay away from them. After Hurricane Andrew, animals from the zoo, as well as a band of monkeys, were on the loose for days.

Because of the myriad of potential hazards, stay inside until you are certain it is safe to go out.

Insurance

Do a rough assessment of your damage: fence, pool screen, cars, roof, and interior damage. Put in a call as soon as possible to your homeowner's insurance carrier to report the type of damage you have. Photograph the damage before you start repairs. Once photographed, you can do repairs that mitigate your damages. For example, if you have a broken window you can board it up. If you are able you can tarp any leaks or holes in the roof. Rain-soaked carpet will stink and mildew if left around until an adjuster shows up. Many people will go ahead and rip it up after documenting the damage.

Power Company

Of course the power company is aware that you have no power. Call them anyway to report live wires if you see any. Also report your location so you can receive periodic updates as to when you can expect your power to be restored.

Trash Pile

Once it is safe to go outside, it is clean-up time. Pick an area of your yard by the street and start to make a trash pile. Put broken branches, wet carpet and other damaged items in the pile. Do not throw spoiled food in the pile. Instead, put it in heavy duty garbage bags and securely tie them so rodents and other animals are not attracted by the odor. Use your judgment regarding how much help your children can safely offer in this job.

Neighbors

Don't forget to check on elderly neighbors or neighbors whose homes appear to have significant damage. Rescue personnel will not be immediately available so neighbors have to depend on each other. If you are able to share water with someone less prepared, do it. The person may not have had the transportation or resources to stockpile water or other items. Be a good neighbor and share.

Life without Power

Just because you may have a generator, don't immediately fire it up after the storm ends. The house will stay air-conditioned and the refrigerator will stay cool for some hours after the storm. Do not give in to your children whining about what game they want to play that requires generator power. Let them enjoy life "unplugged" for a while. If you do use a generator, make sure it is outside in a well-ventilated location to avoid carbon monoxide poisoning.

Phone friends and relatives to assure them you are safe. If you have an emergency situation, call 911. If there is no way to reach 911 or other help, spray paint your roof with a request for emergency help.

Try to make regular meals at normal times. It is easy to lose track of time when you are picking up tree branches or sorting through debris. A peanut butter sandwich lunch can be a good break. Be careful to not overexert yourself when you are cleaning up. Drink lots of water and take regular breaks. Your

goal is to minimize any chance of injury while cleaning up. Wear

gloves and closed-toe shoes.

High-End Items

Some big-ticket items are nice to have after a major storm. One is your vehicle. A high clearance vehicle such as a pick up truck or an SUV is great to drive around after the storm. They are high enough to drive through small flooded areas and can also haul debris or deliver water and supplies to needy neighbors.

The automatic generator is on the wish list of every storm-conscious family. They are large, permanent generators, often diesel powered, which will automatically come on when the power goes off. These cost thousands of dollars and require proper permitting for installation. If you have the money, however, and live in a storm prone zone, you may want to invest in one.

FINAL THOUGHTS

Be Thankful

Remind your family that you love them more than anything that was lost in the storm. Be thankful for your health and the preparations you made. If you are well-prepared and well-stocked in advance of the storm, it gives you the opportunity to help others afterward, instead of needing help.

Learn from Experience

Inventory your hurricane food supply. We routinely use hard to reach cabinets to store canned goods for hurricane season. These should be used and restocked each season. I failed to address this in our house, until our daughter brought it to my attention.

One day our daughter wanted some canned spaghetti, yet our pantry was empty. I told her she could probably find some in the hurricane cabinets. She did, but because the can looked so old, she checked the expiration date on the can. It was ten years old! Horrified, my daughter made a video entitled "Er-Spaghettios" and posted it on the Internet. I was embarrassed by the number of views it received, and have since been more careful about my stockpile of canned goods.

Make notes of anything you wish you had bought to be prepared for the next storm. You can keep a storm journal with notes so the next time you are even more prepared.

Appendices

To Do:

Cash
Gas
Gas cans
Groceries
Bills
Laundry
Charge phones and cameras
Make ice
Turn down air conditioning
Decide whether to evacuate
Prepare outside of home and cars
Decide location and stock hunker down area
Assemble important insurance documents and phone numbers
Photograph house and valuables
Hot showers for everyone
Unplug and cover electronics/appliances

To Have on Hand:

Siphon
Clothesline
Medication
Bug Spray
Trash Bags
Tarps/plastic sheeting
Bottled water
Cereal
Boxed milk
Granola bars
Single serve coffee
Pet food/pet plan/pet crate
Paper plates, cups, napkins, paper towels
Plastic utensils
Bread
Peanut butter
Canned goods
Manual can opener
Propane for grill
Coolers
Buckets
Spray paint
Flashlights
Batteries
Solar charger
Camera
Radio
Important documents

Websites for Weather Information:
www.noaa.gov

This is the official hurricane news presented unemotionally with frequent updates.

www.justweather.com

This has the best models, including radar , the "cone of concern" and the "spaghetti" models which show all possible predicted paths of the storm.